Howard N. (Nicholson) Brown

Sermons

Howard N. (Nicholson) Brown

Sermons

ISBN/EAN: 9783741192289

Manufactured in Europe, USA, Canada, Australia, Japa

Cover: Foto ©Thomas Meinert / pixelio.de

Manufactured and distributed by brebook publishing software
(www.brebook.com)

Howard N. (Nicholson) Brown

Sermons

When the unclean spirit - is gone out of a
^now he walketh through dry places, seeking rest; and
finding none, he saith, I will return unto
my house whence I came. And when he
cometh he findeth it swept and garnished.
Then goeth he, and taketh to him seven other
spirits more wicked than himself; and they
enter in and dwell there; and the last state of
that man is worse than the first.
                    Luke 11. — 24, 25; 26

discussion of evil,— It is a question whose answer [...] I [...] entirely [...] upon the general view and estimate of the character of Jesus,— Speaking for myself I am not disposed to believe that he who stood so entirely emancipated from all the other gross superstitions of his age, was the victim of this— Certainly he used the popular language in speaking of what we call insanity; And whatever power he had [...] by means of his immense personal [...] to rouse the dethroned will and restore it to its rightful place of common [...] called his a power to cast out devils,— But his method of [...] — and his [...] [...] [...] of what was essential and what unessential in his work— will sufficiently explain he literally relieved insanity & in a discussion of the mind of evil spirits,— But some will say no — "This is ___ dishonestly — is no better than lying, if Jesus did not accept the popular notion, and yet purposely used words which led the people to think that ~~~ shared their belief."— People who make that objection ~ this explanation of Christ's language — or the same people ~ just do not ___ ~~~ about ___ phrases or customs or ___, —as if they were very important matters, and I should commend them to the careful study of Christ's life for answers. —

It requires some judgement to discern what it is really worth while to make a fight about, and what might better be left alone.— For example the early quakers were full of whims and crotchets — which they only ___ he ___ by insisting upon.— Doubtless they were as a class singularly pure and good people. but not they largely spent the force of what might have been a tremendous movement, in useless

attacks upon evils for whose remedy the time
was not yet ripe. -- On the other hand, John
Hampden - by throwing himself ... ...
himself in opposition ... ...
... of England, and precipitated the conflict out
which the greatness of modern England has arisen. --
... ... manifested in the ... ... his
... ... seeing when and when to strike, and
when to withhold his hand, - Into whatever issue
... ... with the
superstitious, dogmatic spirit of ... ...
... ... -- But none the less
... ... never ... needlessly stirs up the
... of the people against himself, and though
his ... ... for him,
to provoke him to say something, which would offend
... his listeners, with the rarest skill and
coolness he not only extricates himself from
all ... ... against the

very men who had termed them. — I suppose he will
that
beside other errors and follies with him, this belief in
the possession of devils as a slight matter, — and did not
care to sacrifice any of the time or influence needed
for the establishment of great divine principles — in a [...]
upon his petty superstition, — So we simply adopted
the popular speech, — just as we all use the words
sunrise and sunset, because though not in accordance
with fact, it is not worth while to attempt to [...]
him, — — In this "age" he makes use of the common
belief to enforce my illustration a using point
against his enemies. — — It was the [...]
notion, of Christ's day
that as a people they had expressed all evil
spirits, — Had they lived in the days of their fathers they
would never have worshipped graven images — or put
a prophet to death, — — But here we see that
their virtue is merely of a negative kind, — the
unclean spirit has indeed gone out of him — — a

ceaseless ...... — ... that when he returns he
... find ready entrance, but only so .... but
... other devils .... within ......, so that
its second .... will .... than the first,
this point not only against the ...... I think — but
against the whole ...... civilization — was that
it consisted simply in the abolition of savage ......,
and that .... spiritual life and purpose in
the ...... of single men above the savage
lower, — the ...... would at its highest state
of moral perfection, had simply cast out the evil
spirits of barbarism, — But its moral nature was
so ...... — ...... only having been swept
and garnished. — There had been no growth of spiritual
virtues and power — corresponding with its decline
of savage impulses, — so that it was likely in
.... of ...... and
...... and to sink to lower .... of sin than

History shows how this prediction was fulfilled. The
old civilizations on other ~~~~~~ all ∧ sunk into hopeless
brutality — and expired in ~~ the midst of ~~~~~~ ~~~
~~~~~ riots.— The great Pharaohs of Egypt — gave
place to the luxurious Grecian Ptolemies,— ~~~ you
may search the records of all that is known ~ ~ of
savage life ~ ~~~~ — too ~~~ ~~~~~~ to those ~~~
~~~~~ ~~~~~~ of ~~~~~~ ~~~ ~~~ ~~~~~~ who ∧ successive,
inherited the throne of ~~~~ — (Nero and Caligula) The religion of ~~~~~~
would scarcely afforded the (the) slightest check ~ the decline
of its civilization. Among ~~~ people ~~ the ~~~
religion lent itself increasingly ~ the spread of ~~~~~
tendencies,— ~ Egypt ~~~~~ (did) more ~ debauch
the people, than their religious ~~~~~~,— had even

of sins, which this nation had caught ... with ... Roman civilization. — The ... who ... that Jesus was always thinking of himself and his own mission ... ... mainly ... the sin the Jewish people were about to commit ... putting ... to death. — As if Jesus had said "Your fathers in ... many ... their own prophets; ... how ... now for some while same. — But your ... will return upon you in a ... ... — and you will slay ... the ... of all prophets." — Something of this may ... seen in his thought. ... his words have a much ... meaning. — We know that Christ's native ... of Galilee was at that time filled with ..., through ... with whom Jesus

This illustration of the ~~modern~~ spirit (if such it may be
called) was I doubt not meant to apply quite as much
to the ancient world as a whole — as to ~~any~~ particular
race of the Jews. — — At all events it is capable of
this broad application, and may moreover be used to
illustrate some faults of modern times — which deserve
attention, — . —   It is still more that the views
of our civilization — are worse than the evils which
infest savage life, — From all that we can learn of the
North American indian — ~~before the~~ at the time he
was first brought into contact with europeans. he

in war — but after all — the victims his band how
in inflict were Indians theirs — as compared with
the fiendish outrages perpetrated by the thousands, — He
had not a very clear sense of the laws and rights of
property. — But these Christian Sovereigns who
assumed to give away to their countrymen . lands
that were his by inheritance and to which they had
no shadow of just title, display a much lower
conception of the difference between "mine" and "thine"? —
It was the white man who taught the savage treachery —
injustice — and drunkenness in their worst forms. —
Barbarism does not know how to find its way to
the lowest depths of infamy and vice, till it is shown
the road by civilization, — Now from one point of
view it is a very satisfactory arrangement which enables
the superior race — who cannot cope in strength with
the ... ... to conquer, by planting seeds of vice
among their adversaries — which slowly but surely

part of nature's method or securing "the survival of the fittest." A handful of Europeans land upon these western shores bearing a superior civilization — But neither are they strong enough to maintain themselves against the original occupants of the soil — nor is it possible ... these occupants to their own ... But the laws of the world which make the 'inferior race incapable of acquiring the virtues of the superior, at the same time make the former very susceptible to the vices of the latter — The white man prevails over the red man — by imparting to him those mental and physical diseases — over which he has sufficient vitality to triumph — but which are fatal to the indian — I say — from the purely Darwinian point of view, this is a very beautiful arrangement, — but from another standpoint, it is a very unsatisfactory explanation of the fact that the civilized man exceeds the savage in vice — as much as in virtue, — — — But let us then notice this other thing so often observed in the individual life, — It is by no means uncommon

as we could wish — that even who have from a
fair reputation, who have manifested gentlemanly and
intelligent tastes — and have been thought infinitely above
the reach of vulgar and radical evils, — under some
unusual stress of circumstances — great temptation,
have all but instant and all at once taken on the
faith and treasures of humanity in its most
degraded form, — however uneven the spirit within
them may have been so dealt with, — it is not only
the original — but a legion of devils — which
scatters their souls, and their lost state is unfold
know thou you would have ever dreamed it could
become, — — The gentleman when he stoops is become a
villain, rarely makes a gentlemanly villain, but
almost always transforms himself into a blackguard and
a sot, — . . . . — The explanation of this
may be found in Christ illustration, — The mind

or times have occupied the planes of human experience, and when the mind does roll under said influences — there is nothing in him to oppose their taking entire possession of his soul. — Civilization enlarges the mind capacity. It decorates and adorns the chambers of the soul. — So to speak it prepares apartments them for never minds indeed of one, — and where as is often the case, — these apartments are not strongly manned and guarded by good spirits, — evil spirits easily force their entrance. — In use picturesque phrase than that used by James — we may say that every increase of power or capacity in the human mind, may be occupied and used by bad as well as good influences, and this sufficiently explains the fact that the vices of civilized life are so much worse than those of the barbarian. —

... — That men's minds are often merely embellished and enlarged, without being adequately filled by good purposes. — ... in to ... civilization, is ... some ... and artificial, ... with a certain was ... purely ... — By an artificial civilization — I mean one that grows out of external exigencies and circumstances, rather than internal motives and aspirations. — ... an ... any ... discrepancies ... human justice, — What conscience allows ... by the ... which have us before done the necessity of maintaining ... &c. — "All things are lawful — not all things are expedient" said Paul. — In this practical judgment ... forced to ... the argument — ... "What is ... ?" — ... "What is expedient," — but here ... social reformers go astray. They ... their ideal — it is not ... it is ... impossible ... by it ... life ...

now,— they are for example that ... ... in certain institutions. ... that the law ought to be changed,— But if one, as that ... women as a class the law of which they complain is a safeguard rather than a hardship,— They who make and ... social regulations cannot listen to the claims of abstract justice alone,— and we ought ... meet the ... spirit of ... society— with inclination that things as they are ... heaven's justice, Rather should we admit that in many respects our civilization stands upon artificial distinctions and ... and ...,— and should teach men that to a certain extent these must be employed in ... to have any society at all.— It seems an unjust and cruel thing, that men and wife should

... right enough, — that every ... and other person ... that to break down the present marriage relation would be to destroy ... modern society. — ... not ... the sooner of annulling the marriage contract ... of ... given individual, on the idea that freedom ... him ... her demand it, but because society can only ... the ... power itself, — So I say our civilization is in some particulars artificial, — It has grown not only out of rights and clearer perceptions of ... — but also out of the necessities of our situation. — If man, like the snail — could build his house out of himself, — i.e. if he could express ... in it all his ... and things — it would be the natural outgrowth of his character, — But he must consult his means, —

... ...

... ...

... so ... ... is of course
a mere shell. an empty space swept and garnished
and ready for the reception of evil spirits, that is to say
the duties which this sort of our civilization puts upon
us, - are commanded not by an inward promptings but by
an outward force or necessity, - They are forms which
no true spirit of righteousness can be made to inhabit -
and which therefore are easily taken possession of
by evil forces. ... - There are those forms and customs
which are not the fit expression of the best spirit of
humanity - and there are other forms and customs
which the impulses of a great part of the race have

I righteousness — but in deference to the example set by his feelings — there are two sides to the moral life of the race. On the one side we have the minds of all men forever inspired by God's spirit — which fails for any share left meant by the decay or banishment of evil passions, and is always sounding back the tireless force of the heart. There is a certain very great and blessed truth in that view of human nature which sees in every soul an original and inspired source of moral law. I have so often called your attention to this much — that I trust I have not be accused of leaving it out of sight, when I say that in many — perhaps in most lives — the conscious thought; this original conscious law that is in sustaining the freedom of virtue — its an instinctive tendency to conform

A great many people to say the least _____ — continue in virtuous ways, not because there is any voice in them proclaiming with special _____ the righteousness of _____ ordinary means of duty, not simply because all the respectable world practices their _____, and to omit them or contravene them _____ — would horrify all ones _____ and neighbors, — — Let us _____ themselves we will — the great _____ of men and _____ _____ knows that to a very large _____, — they are kept in obedience to the laws and customs _____ observed by the _____ portion of society — through their _____ _____ and their dread of social obloquy, — This of course means that many _____ minds are — morally _____ — simply empty, — The unclean spirit has gone out of them but no strong spirit of holiness or love has taken its place, — Their conscience being simply _____ so others people do — and _____ the good opinion of those by whom

of those about them, — now I do it wish it be
understood, that into this sort of moral uprightness, to
"even divide" will always tend in any intercourse, because
the trend of social force tend towards to the strongest
of all consciences, — Though the social does not feel keenly
the instincture of uprightness, it does not lead with
weary view — , has of social interacting, — and effective
the temper is as essential as the strongest moral means
to hold the mind free from evil, — And at last this condition
in which men and women only recognize the traditional
claim of honesty and integrity — is very far from
being the ideal condition, — and its special weakness
is that it has no power to maintain virtue in the
midst of adverse surroundings, — Take a man out
of the sober community in which he has been born and
bred — and send him for a time into the midst of
dissipated in social customs, — That will very soon
tell of what manner of stuff he is made, — If

out from the trial is strong as ever, — though for the time being he yields something to the social habits of ~his,

But if he cares nothing for right — save as a means of maintaining respectable appearances, a very brief contact with demoralizing ~~men~~ associates and surroundings will be likely to ruin him for life, — — ~~It is probable~~

We have of course no means of deciding now far people are guided by an interior spirit of righteousness — and how far they simply follow the lead of others in well doing, but I think we must all be conscious of the immense power which social custom holds over us in matters of right and duty, — and when we look out over the world we are made useful that in ordinary times — the standard of morality is kept — when it is, mainly by the force of habit and tradition, now and again in the midst of some grave danger or crisis the conscience of the nation rises to unwonted ~~heights~~ — and ~~~~ the challenge

is the book of my purpose to document
experience, _ forms that will not be told. We
note of it; why moral progress ...
... compared with intellectual growth ...
why the rules of good conduct should
slowly. _ ... the individual mind
from its spirit and conscience have grown
... perhaps cannot be wholly explained. _
... the moral sense is in the spiritual
... capital is in the industrial world, _
... form of human labor. _

designed to contribute to the increase of conscience — which is the golden product of mental endeavor, the spiritual capital of the race, possession of which distinguishes civilization from barbarism. — But it is only by slow degrees that this capital, like natural wealth, can accumulate. — Meanwhile many men & women are not to be _____ for _____. — We are simply _____ the fact that many ____ which conform to the usages of morality are nevertheless almost empty of moral purpose. — We have ____ that the well being of society depends ____ large measure upon maintaining the power of moral traditions — and the practical point I wish to bring out is — that it is our _____ to use the _____ whereby these traditions have been established and maintained in the past. —

I suppose not many things ____ ____ ____ upon the public mind today than a plan for Churches — _____ ____ ____ ____

...in ...... their ....

the ...dit of virtuous living. — The degree of immense
credulity which many men and women of ..-day
manifest in believing that this practice of morals
will take care of itself — is simply astonishing. —
People who make no .... of having any faith in
........, and ...... who somewhat .... placed
themselves as .... in this particular, yet
display a confidence in the essential righteousness of
the human heart — only equalled by those who hold the
.... of divine inspiration in its ....
...... — and unalarmed by any practical views of
life. — — They take it for granted that all men — generally
speaking — will continue to do right just as they will
continue to breathe, whereas that is not to be taken
for granted at all. — Dogberry proved however that
reading and writing "come by instinct"; Then

seems to be a general notion equally unreasonable, that conscience comes by nature,— The truth is that it, one requirement of civilization as much as another — is the result of schooling and schools.— Children will not develop into righteous manhood and womanhood, any more than they will develop into good mathematicians — without training,— — If we want the world to go right we must set for it the fashion of doing right and must uphold the methods by which righteousness is inculcated.— I do not care here to enter upon any argument to show that the Church has been and still is the chief of all agents for carrying forward and upward from age to age the tradition of onwards,— that is perfectly evident to all who look into the matter at all.— The modern world has grown neglectful of Churches — because they themselves have not put forward a claim to any such broad mission as

thoughtful, intelligent individual ~~says~~ says — "I can save my own soul — without any help from the church" which is not enough. — But the individual by himself cannot give to civil the influence toward sustaining and developing the public conscience — that is exerted by an association of _people_ ~~united for~~ united for religious purposes. — That statement I think it needs no argument or illustration, — It is the conclusion which my argument has evidently drawn, ~~true~~ that has been ... if there need, it plain that the public conscience is not self-sustaining and needs support. —

Perhaps some of you will be wondering how I put together the view of moral life here advocated ~~and~~ the opposite institutional view, embodied in my sermon of a week ago, — Well, in truth, it is never an easy task to join together the different sides of a complete statement, — nor is it at all necessary to attempt to decide — how far the world's righteousness is supported by the direct inspiration of God.

to think either out of sight, — — There is a certain
divine voice - in every soul - which we dare not say is
ever completely silenced. — There is in every heart a
germ of spiritual life, which God's spirit nurtures
and sustains, — But the sober truth is, that in
most human lives this spiritual force is very far
from being mature or strong enough to be made
with the entire control of conduct. — — If from an
assurance that God has a foothold in every life we
derive confidence and hope, — the reflection that so far
it is only a foothold which is spread this against
in the realm so widely ruled by human selfishness and
passion, should teach us the practical duties of

all the exterior agencies and influences that "make for righteousness" — The world is yet too young — and the life of humanity is yet far too incomplete, to make 't safe to trust its spontaneous motives and impulses. It is necessary that each one should set his standard of living as high as possible, and should support all that makes virtue outwardly obligatory, in order to hold society to its present moral level, —
The spiritual life — which it is the special mission of Christianity to foster, is surely, if slowly increasing, and we look forward to the time when it shall so completely fill the mind, that the race will no longer be in danger of falling again under the thraldom of unclean or evil spirits. But meantime there is need to surround the growing ——— with every safeguard of pure association, holy precept and example, — every incentive and spur to aspiration and endeavor, that the God has put into our hands or the ———— wit of man can devise, —

Brooklin Mar 9, 1879

Be ye ~~wise~~ ~~harmless~~ as serpents a
harmless as doves.

Matt 10. 16

It seems to be ~~the feeling~~ among people ~~of the~~ world
that to be ^(mostly) religious one must necessarily lack human
virtue. — The religious ~~mind~~ is ~~supposed to be~~ one
which is mostly given up to sentiment. ~~——~~ and which
has little knowledge of ~~the facts~~ purely worldly cares
and interests. — It is said to delight chiefly in ~~glorious~~
~~definitions~~ and is in any ~~kind~~ to confine to
any near and permanent distinctions or definitions. —
Thus, in a recent review of the poetry of the day — some
religious poets being up for gentle castigation it is said
that religious people seldom know poetry of any kind —
~~that~~ they like so sack of sentiment ^(since) in such outrageously
~~ge~~ proportion to this ~~—of~~ that they cannot relish
a ~~—~~ genuine verse. — Again it is said of
George MacDonald and some others of his class, that
they have an air which repels "those who like a
plain answer to a plain question — "Do you believe
it or so". — Now it is a fair answer" continue

I'm not quite sure what I mean, but it is not those ...
other moral and spiritual truths, which
barely must stand on logical propositions or ... ; ...
... to ..., "We believe ... and all the letters of
the alphabet, and all the letters of ... ...,
... is in the clouds somewhere." In so far as this
is a criticism of individuals, — I for one — think that
in too many instances it is only too well merited. —
The spiritual food proposed by a certain class of writers
is of an exceedingly watery kind, — and does not go
far in supply the soul with vigor or strength for the
work of the hour. — — — I lately heard of an Irishman, who
professing to be a good Catholic — still interested in a
public meeting, the methods through which the spiritual
authority vested in the Pope is exercised, on the ground
that instead of repressing the Christian ... ...
... ..., the ...

... it very difficult to ... this ... very ... than the previous revelation. You will understand ... that I am ... no personal ... think my ... that I am not "patronizing." But ministers as a class are looked upon as rather ... intermediates, whose chief business, it is ... consolation - and whose opinion ... any vital question of the hour, is likely to ... ... the ... may ... reserve as higher ... But religion, or at least christianity ought not to be measured by this shortcomings and defects. - It has an immense ... significance ... and its ... and ... ... of religion and the ... ...

have been written of Jesus—? beyond that he
to assume the post which his people had assigned
messiah, and not taken upon himself the political rule
of the Jews.——— More than one great state has sprung
[from] feebler beginnings, and been founded by a much inferior
genius,— as compared with Jesus, Mahomet was
a wild dreamer and a narrow fanatic — yet he waged
a movement — in a deadly [contest] with which —
Christendom only barely triumphed, — and founded a
state which notwithstanding all the great [war of]
distinction [Europe] has [urged] against it, still in its
[decadence] maintains its [grasp] upon the its [ancient]
seats of empire, — — If Mahomet did this, what
might — not Jesus have accomplished, had he
determined to use his great powers in the same [way]
No one who reads his life carefully will find

... possession of those very qualifications — upon which successful men of the world pride themselves, with all his metaphysical tendencies he had a very strong grasp upon worldly affairs, — a very notable faculty for organizing men upon a definite basis for a definite work. — He was of course the founder of the gentile Church, and without doubt the ... of the main distinctive features of ... organization, — the work he did shows) ... is own even a man of great practical sagacity and in his bearing throughout the sorely disputes and controversies with his jewish brethren — we see the .. of shrewdness and bold'ness — of courage and ... which enabled him to guide the new movement into the channels which his own foresight had marked out for it, — — Taking Jesus and Paul as representative religious minds, this line teach the ... of this view that religion is inconsistent teach briefly that men may be at the same time - wise as serpents and harmless as doves. - Christianity does not aim to supplant the generation of strong-willed men-willed and ready-handed men hanamen - with a race of dreamers whose innocence and refinement shall render them incompetent. - It is a misfortune that so many who have the gift of spiritual vision should use that gift only in dealing with speculative problems - and should manifest such entire ignorance of great ethical questions of the hour. - That I say is the world's misfortune - but not the fault of Christianity, for in the person of its founder, and as a matter of fact in his long Christianity has ever been most intimately associated with the conduct of man's worldly life. - People are not better but worse Christians for lacking the powers and feelings which belong to flesh and blood, Then is as you very well

some people to be a mark of high breeding,—
"Of course" they say—"the common people whose business it is to dig and delve—should possess all this practical knowledge. But we the higher order of cultivated intelligence live and move in another sphere." Now every person of sense knows that nobody belonging to whatever station, is any the less a gentleman or lady—but all are in a much higher sense men and women for knowing how ... to turn their hands and their brains to the ... of life's ... affairs,—"It needs a ... man to buy a ... and a ... to make it our ..."

impulses of ordinary humanity — They hold the physical life in contempt — and could how it understood that they never feel the temptations to which human nature are subjects — Now do we not all know that it is a total misconception of the spirit — of Christianity — which has led men to shut themselves up in the monk's living cell and slowly starve to death all human elements of their being? Not less is it a misconception of the kingdom of God on earth which Jesus preached — to suppose that the healthy full-blooded human life is necessarily shut out from it; and that its citizens must in every worldly respect the pale cadaverous ghosts of humanity — Christianity — does not destroy worldly wisdom — ability — or impulses — It makes men harmless as doves not by taking from them the power — nor even wholly the disposition to do evil — but by fixing in their minds a higher disposition to use all their power for righteous and beneficent ends — The ideal Christian

human sympathies and engagements and is lived apart from scenes of ordinary trial and endeavor, — but one which is full of all human instincts and impulses and affections, reduced to the sway of a righteous will. — It is the great feature of Christ's teaching that instead of aiming to destroy those propensities of human nature which lead to the commission of evil, it endeavors to put into the mind a governing power or principle which shall hold them in subjection, — In a disorderly state order may be restored in one of two ways, — either by the extermination of certain classes — or by the growth of a government strong enough to overawe intruding factions, — The method which Jesus chose in dealing with the disorders of the soul — was the latter, — He strove to strengthen its governing faculties — not to destroy any of its subordinate

words - in point of fact Jesus did not lead the life of an ascetic - and his influence did not lead his followers into the practice of ~~asceticism~~ - asceticism, - he surely complained that because he came eating and drinking like ordinary mortals he was called a wine-bibber and a friend of publicans and sinners, - It is perfectly plain that instead of issuing any code of requirements - ~~xxxxxxxx~~ - he tried to fit his disciples to judge for themselves in all special instances what was right, - Therefore I say the true Christian aim is not to destroy any human

leaving men all their ~~poor~~ abil't ~~is do~~ & mischief – renders them homeless & slaves, – I am aware that this is a very broad statement, and one which many will call in question, for there is a very general belief that the world would have been about what it is had Christ never lived and the church never existed, whereas I affirm that Christianity has been the great purifying and ennobling agent in our civilization. I do not mean of course that it is the only religion of the world which has supplied spiritual life – but only that it is our fountain of spiritual influences, –

These comparisons between the religions of different races which have been indulged in so freely of late years amount to little more than a dispute between neighbors as to which ~~has the~~ ~~deepest and purest~~ Deeper and purer well, – Each will continue ~~to draw~~ water from his own well, and each will probably continue to think his own the best,

conceive for the spirit of self sacrifice ~~any~~ ~~~~

any natural genesis ~~out~~ of experience, -- Selfishness can

only beget selfishness to the end of time, - Upon the

selfish use of power there is absolutely no check

in the nature of things - save as one more selfishness

encounters another - and surely it is absurd to

suppose that when two ~~a~~ selfish natures engage

in a deadly struggle for the mastery - either will gain

from the contest an unselfish ~~~~ ~~~~ disposition, - The man

who triumphs is sure to make use ~~of~~ his power

to crush his rival, - His fear will prevent him from

becoming anything but a Tyrant. - The man who

loses is sure to seek every opportunity to overthrow

Some people talk you might think that the physical laws of the world are the great matters of righteousness; why then we may ask do or not these laws check the disposition of animals to prey upon one other? — All the development of animal life from ... to good and from simple to complex has left unchanged the savage nature of the brute creation — No more do they have a modifying influence upon the nature of man, — Suppose a tribe of savages entirely destitute of every philanthropic impulse, and each one acknowledging no check to his selfish desires save his fear of encountering another's selfishness? is it conceivable that such a tribe should of itself develop into a peaceful and orderly society, — Is it conceivable that by unlimited indulgence of brutal passion — men should become merciful? — That by hating their fellows they should come at last to love them? —

acquire an admiration for the acts of brave? — Does not all that we know of human nature lead us to exactly the opposite conclusion, viz that the exercise of evil passions tends constantly to fix them yet deeper in the mind? — And in the world today, do we find that experience teaches the selfish man philanthropy? — If a man enters the business world with a sullen and unscrupulous nature, are there any lessons to be learned in his dealing with men which will teach him kindliness and generosity? — We know there are none. — It has passed into a proverb that trade is selfish, — and men continually complain that the influence of business life so far from softening their dispositions tends all the other way, — The influences about them instead of lifting him toward their ideal — they must fight against in order to maintain their ideal, — And so we see that

inevitably leads to its abuse — unless its possessor
is very strong in resisting the temptations of his
position. — It is not too much to say that it is
impossible to imagine how the natural course
of human experience should have lifted anybody
of them to the reign of usefulness — without there
... voluntary attempt to ... an ideal
... would ... them. — I say it is absurd to
suppose that Jesus could have been born out of
.... a brutal, immoral nation, — absurd to
think that the faintest beginning of the spiritual
influence which culminated in his life could have
arisen from the indulgence of bestial desires. — We
do not gather figs of thistles, in the mental, any
more than in the physical world. The relation between
spiritual and animal existence is not that

his irreconcilable forces his ~~own~~ inclined power which — so far rank as reason or imagination trace them —

Then was a time we suppose when selfish passion acknowledged no check — To day we find a power in the world which does limit the mind in its use of its faculties to good purposes, — Whence has this power come? not out of experience, — for that tend rather to intensify and exaggerate selfishness, — but from spiritual teaching and influences I war with experience, — In saying that christianity is the power which disarms the selfish will, I do not mean of course any body of christian doctrine, or any form that originated with Christ, — I mean that mass of spiritual inspirations traditions and associations — which can be traced away back to the nations out of which the Jewish patriarchs came, but upon which Jesus is left to impress this genius, that henceforth it will bear his name, — I mean that people who to day stand unconnected or very ~~loosely~~ connected with christians — and are

one of a spiritual communion, — only those such a
... receive their fathers and ... before their
own ... — and ... the
... to conform — to follow the ... himself in
example, — — And so a way Christianity. ...
... it make ... to ... worldly wisdom, — is
... has so circulated the use of that
... gained from experience, that it has taught
... as ... as serpents, and as
... as ... — — ... the world must
... to ... Christianity for its continuation of
its work. — Though the influences coming to us from
and through the life of Christ have so largely passed
to the keeping of the church, and find now a
... through secular literature no less potent
... the ... of the Christian ministry, — though

channels, so that there are many spiritual influences playing into our lives not to be readily connected with the establishment of our religion; still there is no man or woman so good or so secure from temptation as not to need to know well the life of Christ. — It has been the fountain of that enthusiasm for righteousness which has led our branch of the human family to its spiritual attainments, and it is still the mark and symbol by which multitudes are guided and sustained in their conflict with evil. — —

Then are many signs of the times which show that society has reached a point at which its continued growth must depend more than ever before upon the strength of those forces which are set or the wisdom which is sent to render it as

that though it apparently comes back again and
again to the same point — in reality it has mounted
from one landing to another of a circular staircase,
and each passage is made upon a higher level. —
Thus — in rough illustration of this truth it may
be said that civilisation is the origin of individual
liberty. To this succeeds the era of great empires — when
the units of society are brought together by
external pressure into an organized whole. — But the
forces of empire fall apart and once more comes an
age of individual freedom — only, through the schooling
of law — men have learned to put their liberty to fuller
use than did their savage ancestors. — This is the
age in which we now are living — an age of
disintegration. — But there are indications that

one long step above barbarism, — ... ... success in
one of coöperation — an equally long step ... ...
corresponding age of empire. — All the causes ... ...
by which the social and industrial world is moulded — ...
illustrates the ... period of independent action — in which
we live. — But side by side with this there are growing
strong perceptions and customs of independence, which
illustrate the more perfectly organized society which our
children will inherit. — — The word coöperation has
become associated with the efforts of labor to free itself
from the domination of capital, — But really the

custom of our fathers ... autumn ... in their
winters' supply of provisions — which for six months
... them independent of the Butcher and Baker, — Now
we live from day to day on what ... functions ... bring
to us, — and a ... snowstorm a thousand miles
away, may ... interfere with domestic economy
in all our homes, — that ... the sort of change
which is ... in every department of
life, — ... commonly ... of private enterprise
... more and more ... the hands of organizations and
... methods of activity, which are all ...
growing with the increase of human needs and the
growth of human intelligence, — Now I say the
... of this new era of co-operation puts into the
                        wise, man
hands of the ~~individual~~ such power as he never
... to disturb the whole framework of
                                                    has
society — and makes a greater demand than ever
~~...~~ was made before upon those forces which bind

While society is composed of states or classes or cliques, each in large measure independent of all the rest, it is not within the power of any one to do serious damage. — But just in proportion as society becomes more perfectly, ^Delicately^ organized ~~as~~ does every crime take on a more terrible and wide reaching power. — The criminal failure of a large business house — which a century ago would hardly have been noticed beyond the city in which it was located, to day is felt in all great business centers the world over, — While therefore it becomes more and more important that men who have the ability to ~~control~~ public interests should ^be Themselves^ ~~also possess the~~ controlled by some power which will ^hold^ ~~them~~ their wisdom ~~to the service~~ of the public well-being,

industries has failed through the rascality of the agents to whom their affairs have been entrusted. There is no remedy for this which can be incorporated into the schemes themselves, — — When you get to the bottom of it, coöperation in every dress — whether in the shape of those systems men occasionally set up — or in the _____ of those wide reaching organizations which grow into shape of themselves, always and everywhere a coöperation must give its agents more power and incentive to defraud than can be found in any private concern, — Its first demand therefore is for honest men, — men who are not only honest in the traditional fashion — but who can bear an increased strain of temptation, without yielding, — — If such men can be found to manage our political industrial and commercial affairs — society will pass over safely into the development, — This I know is a very crude and fragmentary statement of reasons, why to day - more than ever before there is need of binding mens heart's to the sway of holy and unselfish aims — (But it seems so perfectly evident — surely there is slight reason ___ words in trying to demonstrate that our civilization makes an increasing demand for ___ ___ ___ ___ ___ ___ ___ ___ — I ___ ___ to say ___ ___ ___ to repeat that there is nothing in the acquisition of worldly wisdom — which guarantees the uses to which it shall be put. — The higher wisdom which ___ ___ to employ their gifts and acquirements for the good of their fellow men rather than for their own gratifications, this wisdom comes not up from the depths of selfish striving out of which the race is slowly rising — it — comes down to us from those spiritual heights of ___ to which men have not yet climbed, — We do not learn holy living from ___ ___, from the lessons

...ing & righteousness whose _____ and _____ down through the ages to draw our hearts — as the _____ the _____ of the sea, — The world has progres-
ed and very far in some portions, out it has _____ its ancient need to turn to God and _____ whom he has _____, in order that its _____ _____
_____ _____ _____ of moral enthusiasm, as and enlightened by the wisdom which "is first pure" — Devise and plan as much as may, to _____ the _____ that are "out of joint", it all _____ this at last — that the great work of life is up a heavenly kingdom within the hearts of

_____ _____ _____ would will not so, it is accomplished to an _____ end of men, voluntarily, to _____ lives to noble lives — and or strengthen that tide of Christian _____, which slowly _____ _____ _____ _____ all to _____ _____ _____ of

And when he was ... ... a ship, his disciples followed him. And, behold, there arose a great tempest in the sea, insomuch that the ship was covered with the waves; but he was asleep. And his disciples came to him and awoke him, saying, Lord, save us, we perish. And he saith unto them, Why are ye fearful, O ye of little faith? Then he arose, and rebuked the winds and the sea; and there was a great calm. But the men marvelled, saying, What manner of man is this, that even the winds and the sea obey him?

Mat 8 - 23 - & 27.

The ship here spoken of... could have seen of ... only ... all a boat. The little sea of Galilee — some fourteen miles long and about half as wide — was ... in that day like one of our small inland lakes — with ... had boats... and in fishing... and for communication ... the many villages planted thickly along its shores. It is ... it not ... ... a ... ... a ... ... The ... ... And after a fatiguing day of ... ... and his disciples ... for the ... of ... ... in ... side of the lake. He himself ...

frequent or very severe, and his of course ones and to increase the terror of the disciples — when they found themselves caught in this sudden squall, — Though some of their number were fishermen by occupation — and practised sailors — yet they were probably unaccustomed to handling a boat in so rough a sea — and as much frightened as the rest, — In their dire extremity they awoke him and call upon him for help, — Now it would be doing no great violence to probability to suppose that he so [helped] them — not by quieting the tempest, but by stilling their tumult [...] in their own [...] so that they were enabled to take the necessary steps to insure their own safety, — We know how much depends in the time of trouble shipwreck not only upon the coolness and skill of the commander but upon its ability to keep them in full possession of their faculties — so that they can be relied upon to carry out his orders. — We may well suppose that in the confusion and [...] chaos of the moment — the disciples were incapable of extricating themselves from their trail; — that really was to restore courage and order among them; and that the account of his restoring the ... is an addition to the original story for which tradition is responsible. — If we were bent upon finding a ... explanation for all the ... of the ... narrative, this reading of the story of ... killing to ... might very well suffice. — But really it is not ... possibly worth while to attempt such an explanation. — If men ... it — as I suppose we at least all do — that in its passage ... through tradition, the story of ...'s life has been somewhat distorted, all hope of strict historical accuracy regarding ... many of its features is at an end. — How far ... has ... the ... less ... narrative — and what as to ... original ... we can never ... probably ...

with New Testament history — except so far as is
necessary to determine the spirit and ideas of
action in its scenes. — What we now have to
speculate whether it was a miracle — a flash of light
or some supernatural brightness — before which Mr Paul
fell with the ? on his journey to Damascus. — All
we know — and all we want to know, is that, there
was a sudden change came over him, which transformed
him from a persecutor to the chief apostle of the new
religion. — So here it is impossible to do more
than guess, and it is not important to do more
than — what was the actual basis ? in part of
story ? of Christ commanding power over the
troubled waters of Galilee. — The question we will
we are concerned is — Was this miracle ?
as the illustration or person of Jesus ? — This
it can only be that, by showing us how he ?
? in the ? ?

It is become one of the recognized methods of ~~criticism~~ reading both the old and new Testaments, to treat most of their accounts of supernatural occurrences — as growing out of and representing the impressions left upon the mind from action of the prophetic ordering — whatever we may think of this method of interpretation — it any rate it is in much more accord with its probable truth, and is much more satisfactory to all lovers of the Bible than the myth... theories put forward by the ... and the ... school. — These theories go a long way ... to explain how such stories were evolved in the ... occurrences of a people — But not ... need — we may ... to show how ... might ... to ... what ... they ... upon the ... and might ... by showing that these imaginations were actual reality — that ...

...mon level of humanity in virtue and ability
to they have seemed almost belong to another race
... common race... It is ... more reasonable to
... that wholeness of imagination that ... a
... history is due solely to the exaggerations
... distortions which arise from looking at any
considerable distance through the twilight of memory.
Meanwhile even these exaggerations ... help, in
much aid us to a better understanding of the
... of a ... like ... they ... as that
... and attitude of this nature ... the ...
impression upon the mind of this age, — Thus the
way of his ... in ... ... with a few
... figure — may indicate the remarkable
... ... to ... a ... of ... ...
...

... ... which
finds the ... of ... — This ... is expand
... common ... of ~~...~~ experience into sublime
and inspiring truths must have strongly ... itself
... the attention of Christ's Disciples, and we
... ... suppose that in ~~the~~ an age of allegory,
... attempts ... ... by
means of ... pictures — some conception of the
... ... in this respect — would lead to
the formation of this story of a miraculous feast. —
At all events — I repeat — the question, whether or
not Christ did feed the five thousand as reported — or
whether or not he quieted the raging tempest at
a word, are comparatively of slight importance to
us, beside ... ... question — what these recorded
incidents tell us of the character of the man. —
In earlier times men thought it essential to

the greatness of Jesus - that he should ~~possess~~ a
power of command over the ~~forces~~ of nature. - The
modern world however - more and more ~~finds his~~
true greatness in his spiritual perfections, and holds
a decreasing interest in miracles, ---

It is evident ~~that the~~ writers of our Gospel found
the point of this story of Christ silencing the storm. which
had become current in their Day - in the exclamation of
the disciples - What manner of man is this - ~~that even~~
~~the winds~~ and the sea obey him. - They were astonished
at the display of authority. - It certainly presents a
striking picture to the imagination, - this majestic human figure
standing ~~in the~~ prow of the half submerged boat and
by ~~the might~~ of his will compelling the angry elements
to ~~subside~~ into calm. - But after all is the picture
any more ~~stirring~~ than that of the same figure
towering above a turbulent sea of human faces -
over which the strong winds of passion were

common anger to break into perfect silence? — And this scene was enacted again and again. — What an [?] of the nature of the people and the time. — the strong national feeling of the Jews rebelling against the Roman [?], the constant rise of fanatics who stirred up [?] strife — the bitter hostility of [?] contending [?] — all that we can gather of the [?] and [?] of the period, shows us how much is contained in the oft recurring [?] of the gospel — "They sought to kill him" — and how much is conveyed in his other saying "But he passing through the midst of them, went his way" — Day after day in his teaching — as the Pharisees sought to entangle him in his talk, [?] scenes of [?] disorder must have arisen. — We must remember that there was no [?] of habit or association to enforce silence among the audiences he was accustomed to address, composed of many who were indifferent to him or hated his doctrine - as well as of those who sympathized with his teaching, - Nothing but the magic of his eloquence could hold the quiet attention of such a motley collection, and as many of his utterances were directly opposed to the beliefs and prejudices of a great part of his hearers he must have been often assailed with a din of vehement protest and questioning, - It could not have been otherwise than that his audiences should have broken time after time into a perfect babel of uproar and confusion, - This was the kind of storm in which he continually lived and which he had to face day after day, - Day after day he stood in the presence of an angry mob which would gladly have taken his life, and "no man laid hands on him." That he continued his work for years in spite of the fierce hatred of his foes - shows him to have possessed a wonderful power of command

imagine as often as his language ... a
clamorous ... the voices of this
evening rose like the howling of a tempest - and
the surging throng began to press with overwhelming
force upon the little band of disciples gathered
about their master - as great waves bear down upon a
laboring ship - how the voice of Jesus would go out
over the multitude - rebuking its violence and
commanding peace - in tones whose authority was
not to be resisted, - May it not have been that
the disciples in describing such a scene as this
would liken it to the sudden stilling of a storm
at sea - and that thus from metaphorical winds
and waves, grew up in the second or third generation
after him a belief that he had found literal
winds and waves to obey him, - It seems to be the
inevitable rule that the seed of spiritual truth
dropped in a great mind - must sink into the

many years before it can spring up and blossom in after time, — It is not strange therefore — and is no impeachment of the substantial truth of the narrative that these memories and impressions of [...] should have taken a material dress. — Indeed during the ages ⚹ which were incapable of appreciating spiritual emotions, men would not have cared enough about the record of Christ's life to have preserved it — unless it had worn this cloak of the marvellous. — ~~And~~ But now that men can begin to appreciate the real beauty and sublimity of his nature — we may ~~take up~~ throw this cloak aside — to reveal a divinity which manifests itself not through arbitrary interference with natural law — but through the wisdom purity and love which are the truly regal and divine attributes of being. — — — It is plain that Jesus did speak to men "as one having authority." and that his very presence had an air of command — To which

his ~~career~~ career — concerning which there is no question —
This is I suppose was one of the facts about him which
made a very strong impression upon the minds of his
disciples — and when we find such a story as this, of his
turning storm into calm — it only seems to impress
our estimate of that authority ~~which~~ for which men
could only find expression in words. by likening it to
a power of control over the winds of heaven, —
... I suppose ~~that~~ the story was originally a kind
of allegory which through tradition lost its spiritual
significance and came to be literally believed — and
that is its present form — it testifies to the power
with which christs authority stamped itself upon
the memory of his immediate followers, — —

Now it has been made the basis of some criticism
of the life of Christ — that he did assume so much
authority — that he set himself up as a master —
and claimed as his right the adherence of his
disciples, — — But this criticism is entirely disposed

lay revealed very plain facts concerning the nature and scope of the authority which he exercised, — In the first place instead of pushing himself forward in a place of command — he simply took what position his welcomers freely accorded him, and was ever at continual pains to prevent them from setting him upon too high and absolute a throne, — At the outset of his career he determined to abandon the temporal aims and ambitions of the long expected Jewish Messiah, and his oft repeated injunction to those whom he had helped — "that they should tell no man he was the Christ" betrays his repugnance to having his name connected with the political expectations which in the Jewish mind centered about that office — He did not choose to be a king and fought against the disposition of his friends to make him king, — There is good ground for believing that the chief reason why Judas betrayed him — and the priests finally gave him over to his enemies — was that he would not [ ] place and

make himself king — Their real cause of offence
was that he would not be made king, — No good
was great enough for Roman pride, to a prospect in
setting over its offenders, — She sent all they could have
can got is now seen to us of the head of an army
strong enough to drive out the invaders, — But he could
not be raised to such a command — and therefore his hands
be strong true him, — he offended his Countrymen not
by claiming too much authority — but by refusing what
they were eager to invest him with, — — ¶ When
a soldier hailed him first — master, — he replied "There is none
or not king," when another besought him, "Master
art thou my brother, that he denied the intention with
an" ——— — "who made me a judge or a
"Do over thee?" — So that his authority did not
as often a basis of self-assertion, — so far was he
from thinking himself its notice as an oracle or

obedience men are seeking to render him. -- It is evident therefore that what authority he did exercise - was in no sense fictitious - but such as superior intelligence must always hold over inferior minds. - He was a Master - because those who listened to his teaching and felt the his greatness of soul - freely yielded him that title, - Not only the ignorant multitude - but the rich and great in whose houses he was a welcome guest addressed him as their superior - and hung upon his utterances - as on the words of one much nearer than themselves to the infinite source of wisdom. --- And this was the secret of his power to control the turbulence and storm which his teaching often provoked, - However his calm statements of the broader truth - might offend the bigotry of his hearers; however his scathing denunciations might awaken the fierce anger of superiors and oppressors - they could no more escape the sense of Christ gravitation. — In the very onset of this world they were forced to acknowledge the divine power of the word which burned into their souls, — and inflamed as they were with passion, they dared not touch heaven's messenger. — Concerning him it may be said — What — the mouth of the Danish monarch was only an empty word. "There's such divinity doth hedge a king, that Treason can but peep to what it would — acts little of its will." — There is something in the eye of man upon which the most savage beasts have even known to quail. — With all this thirst for blood to drive him on — even lions and tigers may be held in subjection by the mysterious gleam of authority which their instinct can perceive shining out from an intelligent human soul. — — So the savage natures of men — rebel at least as much as they may — are ever awed by the divine light which at the same

which is qualified to strike down the form which
incarnates the majesty of God's own. — A weight as of
iron holds down the feet which start forward to trample
upon the embodyment of divine authority, A spell
as of magic holds the guilty heart in silence before the
pure image it would fain destroy, and compels it to
listen to the accusing words which fill it with rage,
Though men hate the Christ — and gather about him in
crowds — with stones in their hands to kill him. —
still time and again he passes through the midst of
them — and no man dares lay hand upon him. —

This wonderful authority. cannot of course be
wholly traced to any single source among mental
faculties, — It belongs rather to the full and complete
perfection of all attributes of personal being. — It
cannot be gained by the mere philosopher however fine
his logic may be — nor by the good man who is not
at the same time wise. — nor by the soul, full of

...ral principle. — It belongs with what we call manhood. — the full combination of all noble qualities. — But more than any other single attribute or faculty, this quantity may a raise I think to moral purity. — This coupled with an unswerving moral courage — is sure to compel respect. The rabble are always overjoyed to find a man who is not afraid of them, and for this alone are inclined to fall down and worship him. — The demagogue discerns this weakness of human nature — and works upon it. — Though at heart the veriest coward, he learns to assume the air of bravado. — and can confidently count of our winning applause, by an appearance of courageous resistance to reigning opinions. — But very different is a tribute which ... pays to the intrinsic strength of genuine worth. —

which holds in any case how ... it loves men — and is entirely given up to the great purpose of putting right in the place of wrong. — Such a soul does not know what fear is. — It cares so little for self — and so much for truth that it never thinks of its own dangers. — The secret of the power of Jesus was that he was not in the least afraid of his enemies. — In love ... every ... even when their hatred and fury ..... the highest pitch, and never for an instant quailed before them. — The courage itself surrounded him as a wall of protection, — But such courage is only born out of moral strength and purity. — So that we come back to his moral perfections as the great source of his authority. —

And in the world at large this is the only basis of real personal power and rule. — The great value of Christ's life is that it so symbolizes and illustrates the life of humanity. — Other great lives show us special features of or faculties of the mind. A man

... life of men ... through him ... and to establish ... the ... of human ... which have ... his personal authority may ... us. upon ... personal authority ... must stand, — — — It may ... as ... to secure social order, ... numerous ambitious spirits seize upon these ... thinking chiefly to acquire Dominion, — the ... soul ... which ... wield ... and ... — What was Pilate ... all the power of the Roman state ... and a supple ... in the robes of office — ... but it was ... this ... for Calvary, — who ... does so little of his own ... or is present ... air of others, as sword and 'lording above the commander of Rome's resistless legions, is after all the real king of the Army. — He is the man who bends the sword to the sway of his will — whose authority lives and grows — long after the throne of the Caesars has ceased to be a seat of empire. — So everywhere and in all times — official station of itself does not confer the power to rule men. — The man who wears the imperial crown — may be the most abject slave to be found throughout his dominions. — In office or out of office it is always a question of the man. — And that soul ~~[illegible]~~ carries with it the greatest power to enforce its will upon other minds — which most nearly approaches the Christlike pattern of moral supremacy.

It is the attractive power of a moral ideal which above all other forces draws the heart of humanity. It is the weight of moral conviction which gives

of moral purity ~~and they~~ they will sooner or later yield to its control — as they will yield to nothing else. — Despite all the instances in which the eyes of the populous are dazzled by the merely external pomp of political leaders, — All tending to the statement that "no person can acquire great or permanent influence in the affairs of nations or neighborhood, ~~~~ by means of any other than that moral force which appeals to the divine authority ——— ———. It may often happen that the real leaders of society stand in the background, and that titular dignitaries or dull official officials seem to hold command. But sooner or later you find the man who ~~shapes the opinion, and~~ ——————— ——————— ——————— there are but few ——————— ——————— which can ——————— his highest place in history, — — —

In this democratic age, there is ———

. — So it has in a certain sense — though in a certain other sense the authority of the individual is just as important a factor of human life, now as it was in the days of Cæsar or of Charlemagne. — — The process of levelling the outward conditions of men which has gone so far will probably go much farther, — The holders of rank and fortune, are made to assume more and more the attitude of public servants. — Worldly station becomes less and less the station of leadership, — In a certain way the dream of communism is coming true, for though wealth is still held, and must continue to be held by individuals, — yet its possessor as time goes on — finds himself held by increasing responsibilities to the position of steward of public trusts, — But the whole dream of communism never can be realized, for no process of levelling can break down the eternal distinctions between high and low — good

but let them set what laws they please from their
stated rules, they can neither ~~cannot~~ abolish that royalty of
soul which moral superiority imports — nor interfere
with its exercise of _____ — The world must
have its leaders to day — as much as ever — only they
are not always known by outward insignia — There
is a great change in the method of conducting warfare,
since the day when the King led his army in person —
and was known all over the field by his resplendent
armor, — Now the commander in Chief — is never
seen upon the battle field, yet an army is no
more self-directed than in the age of Chivalry —
that you would go some miles away from the scene
of combat, to find in — very likely the plainest dressed
member of a group of officers the man whose will
the movement of ~~the army~~ a great army, — — So the
progress of events tends continually to abolish men
_____ distinctions, but it cannot do away ~~with~~
with — and indeed tends rather to ~~app~~ extend the

authority of the truly great human soul, —

It is at first an appalling ~~thought~~ when we remember how completely all the high interests of society, lie at the mercy of the mob, ~~&~~ if once the mob rises in its brute strength, — I do not wonder ~~that~~ people are frightened at the phenomena of socialism, and look ~~with dread~~ to the restlessness of ~~those~~ Titanic forces, which have so often ~~oppressed~~ society, — But if ~~they who~~ are at the top of the ~~social~~ scale are there by divine right, and are exercising a ~~divine~~ authority — there is really little ~~to fear~~, — We continually go back to the French revolution in our ~~reasonings~~ and ~~dread~~ a ~~recurrence~~ of its scenes, — But the ~~trouble~~ then was — that when passion arose there was no Christlike authority to ~~confront~~ it, — They who ~~held~~ in ~~reins~~ of ~~men~~ a ~~power~~, had ~~mani~~

... , — let us keep in mind this picture of ... ... the angry elements ... ... ; and let us ... ... that in so far as we can embody his moral strength and ... ... — a hold a power of certain command over all the turbulent spirits of this ... , —

let us ... ourselves too that all human authority ... ... , — Man rules, by entering into ... ... — and ... somewhat of the infinite power ... ... the universe, — — The nature of his authority knows is the nature of that limitless power that is ... above all, — — As man by virtue of his limited ... ... — ... the savage instincts which oppose ... ... the righteousness of God prevail against all ~~... ... ...~~ he has ordained, — If we cannot trust ... ... command over ... ... , and I ... that in the infinite holiness ... ... there is always ... to subdue the

Yea: if thou crust after knowledge, and lifted
up thy voice for understanding; if thou seekest him
as silver and searched for her as for his treasures;
then shalt thou understand the fear of the word and
understand his knowledge of god.

Prov. 2. — 3, 4, 5.

A new method has of late come into use, to
characterize a certain position in thought, which
heretofore has looked in .... some. — Those
.... have .... knowledge ...
... . of ...., ... have denied ... ...
any right of certainty regarding final causes, have been
generally known as the positive school. — In choosing the
name ... perhaps sufficiently well chosen. — The founder
of this school ...... to stop ... be regarded as endless
and profitless speculation — and to confine thought to
objects regarding which we can have positive knowledge,
He desired that his methods should be used for ....
purpose and to establish certainties, therefore his system is
.... "positive". — But in point of fact, his followers
have used his system, and have made it the ....
.... point of their own writing — to show not that
... a .... known — but what must ....
remain unknown. — — The exigences of ....

what others profess to know — rather than
possess any special curiosity.

In the early history of the Church, there arose a very large and powerful sect of men calling themselves Gnostics, who professed to know all about spiritual things. The modern agnostic, on the other hand, is one who denies mans power to know anything of spiritual things, — and both in literature and practical affairs his influence today is almost as widely felt as was that of Gnosticism in early Christian society. —

Now while I do not propose to go into any detailed account of this agnostic phase of thought, there is one special feature of it to which I desire to call your attention. — They who have arrived at the conclusion or justification — superstitious. — That word superstition constitutes for them a whole and convincing argument against religion. — for of course they say every superstitious idea must be bad in its influence. — We must certainly admit that many degrading theories and practices have crept into religion — and still abide there. — We cannot deny that men continue to reason to know more in can — known — and more than it is good for them to assume to know. — But still, from the agnostic standpoint, the question whether any given belief is up to a good or bad influence over practical life — is altogether distinct from the question whether that belief is superstitious, and he has no right to roll these two questions into one — by assuming that the whole problem of practical lives is solved — in declaring all or any of the beliefs in spiritual realities to be without foundation

accepts the christian theory of morals can set up an absolute standard of right - which is the standard of utility, - We who occupy the christian position - can say that affirming the ... to any belief is equivalent to pronouncing it evil, - We can affirm that whatever is false in fact, must necessarily produce evil results, - Because we set the moral law above all questions of utility, - We do not wait to see what is the practical working influence of an idea, - we need only ask - is it true or false? But the agnostic on the other hand - professes to leave ...

That without it the race comes sparsely & miserable. In saying that God is unknowable - agnosticism does not pronounce against the value of theological belief. — In order to be self consistent — and faithful to its own methods, the school of thought must show upon empirical or experimental grounds that religious ideas are hurtful or fail to do good; — before its claim to superior mind is to everything now in ... ; — We may meet the agnostic upon his own ground — with the claim that whether we have any knowledge of God or not — it is practically wiser to pretend that we have such knowledge and he cannot answer . ...

not to the influence of any ...... beliefs. — If men
had brought .... about it .... think ...d
.... influence, — But war has been
the ....
.... so that religion is not responsible for the
brutality of .... — On the contrary it has ....,
so far as ...... a ...... — It was the priest-
... held back the murderous hand of .... christian,
called even kings to account for their bloody deeds —
and opened to the hunted and oppressed a sanctuary
which the cruel hunter of his own prey did not
dare to violate. Though religious fanaticism — has been
capable of perpetrating a massacre of St. Bartholomew,
still, nothing is plainer than that the spirit of
religion is .... has ....
.... — So ......
.... — There is
.... in politics — in art, — ......

...of a special weakness of religion. — It is unjust and fanatical in the last degree to hold Christianity responsible for all the doings of Christians. — The entire unreasonableness of the charge — may be inferred from the fact that they who make it — often — in the same breath call the Church a mere cypher in common affairs, and ascribe to it this vast power — among men against each other in the fiercest hostility. — The truth is that during the middle ages — when its power is most complained of — the Church was almost a cypher, — so far as any original Christian influence of its own was concerned, — At the

of this it has been gradually deprived. — But it is
... of Christianity on the other hand, that its authority
was very ... in the days of ... ... and
that its power has constantly grown — as the temporal
... of the Church has gone ... decay. — So that
the ... and crimes ... committed in the
name of religion, are in no sense the result of
religious influences. On the contrary the historic point at which
religion begins ... its ... of formalism and ...
... into the intellectual life, is the point at which
... begin to disappear. — If we were to
... what the agnostic declares — viz. that religious
beliefs are a mass of superstitions, still we could
claim ... on the whole the world stands largely

accusation. We may not only claim with some confidence — that experience shows him to be practically no wiser than they who believe. — But we can go a step farther, and declare that he is less wise, — that (still leaving unsettled the question whether it is possible to know anything of God) they who persuade themselves that they have such knowledge — have a much clearer insight into the sources of human happiness, than they who will not try to convince themselves of the existence of Deity. — Bear in mind that we are still looking at the world, and speaking from the Agnostic standpoint. — He is entitled only to consider, what makes this life worth living. — The subtle way in which an affirmation of divine realities creeps into many a formal denial of their existence is very instructive, — Here for example we are found asserting

... being of his mind. — There is no necessity for
... their illusion, and it ... ...
keep it up. — When a man declares that he must
follow ... ... his consequences whatever they may,
he is a ... — He thereby assumes to ...
something which ... experience. — He shows that
fundamentally he stands upon a religious faith, and
if they who ... saying to-day — "there is no God, but
it is a sorry truth — a we must follow the truth," —
will compel ... the affirmation that has crept
into their denial, they will find it to contain all
the essential ... of religion, —— But ...
... ... simple — is one who
recognizes no higher duty than that of securing
... happiness, — ... ... he thinks

himself so wise, in ridding himself and others so far as possible from the sway of religious ideas — yet judged by his own aims he is foolish and short sighted. — A loud protest is sent up — when the Christian Moralist declares that the belief in future rewards and punishments is necessary to support the practice of virtue in this life. — Man is not so ignoble it is said as to need to be brought over to the side of honesty by the hope of future glory — and many heroic lives are instanced, which have been unsupported by any hope of life beyond the grave. — Still notwithstanding these individual cases. I take leave to affirm that the average man is not so noble a creature, that he can dispense with his expectation of future joy or pain, and live above the selfish and brutal passions with which his heart is stocked. — However let that pass. — At least it will not be denied, that in order to live

meaning. — We shall not take much heart or courage for anything above the enjoyment of the moment — while we seem to be only longer motes — dancing for a little longer moment in sunshine or shadow — and then disappearing forever — having served no purpose — and left no permanent gain, — — — There is no time now to discuss the various meanings — with which agnosticism seeks to invest human life, — But let us glance at the highest aim which the agnostic proposes — that of "living into the life of humanity." — There is a certain _____ heroism in ___ devoting oneself to the happiness of the millions yet unborn — at first very attractive, and seemingly sufficient as an incentive to high endeavor, — But the insufficiency of this aim lies in the fact that it does not ___ escape the limitations of time, — and furnishes no means

inevitably come to an end, and when that end is reached - be it ten years or ten thousand years away, all that has preceded it is vain and meaningless, unless its results pass ~~over~~ into new realms and cycles of being. - He who works simply for the good of man here upon this earth, is but piling up a mound of sand, of which the winds and waves of time will at length obliterate every trace, and the certainty that fate shall at length render all his labor in ~~f~~ vain, must rob him of enthusiastic devotion to the aim he has chosen. - The coral insect - had it more intelligence - ~~might~~ might adopt as its purpose this of "living into the life of its race." As it ~~lays~~ the foundations of its structure - it might think that others building upon its tomb - would be lifted a little nearer the light of heaven, - And as the last generation of busy workers, having brought ~~the~~ its rocky tenement up to the surface of the ~~waves~~, ~~say~~ the work of ages reared, and ships would find refuge from storms within its enclosing harbors. — With him thoughts the coral world might assume itself that its work had not been in vain — But there comes one day an earthquake shock — which plunges the island fathoms deep beneath the waves, — The patient labor of centuries is entirely brought to nought — and all is as if that busy reef race had never lived, — Now can we imagine any intelligence looking forward to such a catastrophe, lying in wait to destroy every trace of its ever having lived and worked, and not losing heart in its undertakings? — Such a gulf of ruin, we all know

swing through space a desolate and burnt out planet
like the moon, — then of what avail will it have been
so far as agnosticism can tell us, that you and I now
live noble lives and die heroic deaths? — One may consent
to die and be forgotten — if his work can live, — But if that
too must ultimately perish like "the baseless fabric
of a vision," what meaning can we find in the trials
and labors we are called upon to face? I do not say
that the spread of agnosticism would lead people to commit
suicide. — Experience shows that men may believe existence to
be the worst of evils and still cling to it as ardently as
anybody, — But I do say that the highest aim it can set
before the mind is unsatisfactory, — and that men will
not work for future ages — knowing that thereby they
are only writing their names in the sands of the sea-shore
as they will serve an Eternal God, who never
never suffers the results of righteous effort to be

little difference whether the final work of earth be only a few years or many ages away;— So long as we know that all things human must come to an end,— and are ignorant of any way by which the life now in us may escape to other realms— carrying with it the results here won,— — Agnosticism makes loud professions that it finds as much joy and enthusiasm in doing good as anybody.— No doubt— after the motive power is shut off— the ponderous wheels continue to revolve quite a time before losing their momentum,— But when you shut the mind out from belief in God. you do cut off the motive power which has for ages supplied men with hope and courage,— and gradually moral activities will lose their force.— To teach men that they can know nothing 'above this present material existence is to pluck from this life the central heart of its meaning,— and to strike a fatal blow at all noble peace and satisfaction, — —

as he *foresees*, — unless it be wisdom to turn *within* us
into *soul wholly* — and substitute *despair for hope*, — He
ought to see, that in accordance with his own method
of *reasoning* — it is foolishness in him to *attempt to*
discredit faith, though faith is in his *estimation* only
another name for *superstition*, —

So far I have *tried* to judge *agnosticism* from its
own standpoint. *Let us .... us take our ....*
position — and look at it through our own eyes, — — what
of this dogma — which modern *thought* has so confidently
proclaimed — that God is unknowable? — I do not
propose to plunge you into a metaphysical discussion,
but only to take up the counter assertion of his *text*
that they who seek — as for his treasure — *shall understand*
the knowledge of God, — — You often *hear* it said that
people must believe what they can — not what they
would like to, — and while there is a certain truth
in this *remark* — as it is too *often* used — it is

...dreaded to try to force ourself into a belief with or against the impulsive deductions of reason, — to ... more careful in forming any permanent ... and ... or ... it. — When we go to the ... would seeking support for a belief we have already fashioned, the temptation is strong — to shut our eyes to some facts — and to ... others into compliance with our designs. — But this is a temptation from which nothing can free us. — It is utterly impossible ... the mind drift with ... chance currents may take it, spite of everything ... we all have fancies and dreams which we should like to see proven true,— as we shrink from seeing a disagreeable person thrust into our society,— We dread the necessity of giving up some cherished belief—as we dread the loss of a friend,— Talk in as high sounding terms as we please about not being afraid of the truth, this is the inevitable case with all of us, from which no system of philosophy can set us free,— every mind is forced to do some theorizing, and every mind decidedly prefers that what it believes to be true — should be the truth,— — So that all we can do to prevent this warping of judgement which results from bending fact to fancy — is to put the individual mind upon its guard.— — No thinking person will drift aimlessly about on the tides of thought — without effort to shape his or her own course.— Nor is it desirable that people should do that,— and the fallacy covered by this

...des and currents of thought to make our way toward ... fixed Conclusion. — It is not only perfectly proper to do this — it is unavoidable not to do it, — Though the mind which sets out — desiring to find proof of the existence of God is sometimes tempted to make a ... use of facts, still it is perfectly justified in ~~wishing~~ to find satisfactory support for religious faith and may do so without dishonest dealing with ... realities, — They who seek the knowledge of God as men seek for his treasures — do find ... probability ripening into certainty. — Agnosticism has ~~not~~ made such studies toward Dominion, not because of any inherent weakness of faith, but simply because men have been too busy — or too ... with prevailing views, to seek the

The skepticism of the day is partly the result of aimless drifting. — The Church has not taught them to think for themselves — but has encouraged them to entrust their thinking to the minister or priest. So when the minister and priest fail to satisfy their reason, instead of looking into religious problems for themselves — they simply let them drop, No wonder that they cease to know God, for though there is a certain natural and instinctive faith, which grows up in the heart without effort, still no belief in God can have much virtue or strength, till it has acquired a strong hold upon the intellect. — We must seek knowledge of God, as we seek other knowledge — in order to have any clear or certain understanding of his ways. — The trouble is not so much lack of means for assuring ourselves, as lack of disposition to use the means — and seek the evidences through which religious certainties are to be found, ——

Then again, not a few people who are loudest in their declarations against the idea of forcing relief — have unreasoningly forced themselves into non-relief — which surely is just as bad. — They have grown impatient with the unreasonable notions, which the religious world so publicly indulges, — and in this _____ _____ them themselves against all its _____, — — Out of this rebellion has grown a belief that the whole of religion is nonsense, — they _____ a _____ sin to ourselves all faith, and have sought only the evidence of the unreality and impossibility of religious ideals. — It is not strange that such _____ should succeed in convincing themselves that God is only a myth. —

The fact that people who do not seek at all or seek in the other direction, is certainly not proof that they who search for, a reasonable basis for faith, _____ a disappointed, — On the contrary — the idea of _____ _____ _____ the _____ _____ by all our habits and methods of thinking - that any earnest quest for knowledge of him - is ... ... — If thou criest after knowledge! - If thou seekest her as silver, and searchest ... her as for hid treasures! what else can mortals do, who have any appreciation of the facts of their situation — any feelings or tastes above mere animal gratification? How can men and women content themselves to live on day after day - with the great mysteries and uncertainties of existence brooding over them - and without one single gleam of hope in anything above the level of their daily experience - or beyond the few years of mingled pain and sorrow granted them on earth? They do not content themselves with this — Beneath all their careless gayety, and their eager absorption in life's work them lies a dull pain, which fills them with discontent human nature is enjoy life divested of all religious hope and faith,— The great logician — who has been supposed to be entirely destitute of the belief held of his fellow-ries, and the world discovers that down in his secret heart he always cherished a hope that life might be something other than his logic had painted it,— That hope in the Everlasting wisdom, feeble though it may be — is the source of all the peace a human soul can know,— Without that — love — conviction — even Deity itself are only fleeting dreams which make the mocking unreality of life more terrible by only concealing it,— He is the fool who in the name of wisdom — seeks and finds himself from such emptiness of heart,— He alone is brave who strives to hold his own with the everlasting certainty, that the love and favor of an infinite God rule over us,——

Brooklin Nov 30. 1879

Charlestown April 1879

The next day John with Jesus
and saith, Behold the Lamb of G—
the sin of the world —
John

It is somewhat remarkable — all things considered — that throughout the new Testament, so little use is made of the comparison between Christ and the Jewish sacrifice for sin. — — The resemblance is sufficiently striking to lead us to expect, that in an age when language was so largely made up of symbols and comparisons — the disciples *speak of the* would be full of references . Jesus as the atonement made for the world's sin, but in point of fact these references are almost wholly confined to two *viz.—* books — and those of doubtful authenticity — x the epistle to the Hebrews, and the so called Revelations of St John, The weight of authority is *now* decidedly against the opinion that the epistle to the Hebrews was written by Paul, and the book of Revelations is so entirely different from the rest of the new Testament that nobody knows just what to make of it, — In the Acts of the Apostles — the doctrine of

The resurrection of Christ is the great theme then constantly wrought constantly forward. It is this which Paul makes the point of his speech before Agrippa — and it is by preaching this that Stephen is led into that controversy with the ears which ends in his martyrdom. --

The death of Jesus had in the thought of his followers a double significance. — It freed them from some burden which they had inherited and borne in the past, and it also opened before them new certainties and hope for the future. But it was this latter meaning which at first chiefly engaged their attention. — In the gospels it is made plain that the early disciples considered Christ's triumph over the grave — the highest of all his achievements. In this thought he died — not so much for the purpose of removing the world's guilt — as that he might rise again the third day, (and show them the way to heaven) So in all the undoubtedly genuine epistles of Paul — the great truth which

from the dead and became the firstfruits of them that
slept. — It was not till later that Christians recognized
with strongly the other meaning of Christ's death —
out of which grew the doctrine of the atonement (in its dogmatic form.)
Still, though it was overshadowed by the new hope
of immortality brought to light — there was in the
minds of the first Christians, a perception that
Jesus had (through his life or death) paid some penalty
or removed some load, which had hitherto borne
heavily upon them, — but how much was
meant by such expressions as this which John
said, "Behold the — lamb of God." it is impossible to
determine, — Certainly the writers of the new testament
had no such fixed doctrine of the atonement as
was developed by the later church — Their language
is figurative — and they employ so wide a variety of
symbols, that it is impossible to reduce this
to the more units of a definition

The disciples being Jews — and familiar with all jewish customs and ideas — would naturally use the terms of their old faith. — ... in preaching the new dispensation, — How far they had definite theories of an atonement made by Christs' death, and how much more than mere figures of speech are their references to the blood of Christ which cleanseth from sin, it is difficult to say. — In all probability, however, they meant little more by such phrases, than the general purifying influence which Christs' life and death had ... exerted. — But

an infinite God. — Therefore man's guilt is infinite. — The "therefore" it is true has no place there, — but one soon gets used to finding the word ☒ in unexpected places. — if one has much to do with the writings of old school theologians, — Having established man's infinite guilt, if it follows that infinite satisfaction must be made, — Only an infinite being can meet this demands of justice. — Therefore God took upon himself human likeness and in the form of man — paid the debt of suffering — which only an eternity of woe on the part of his children, could have discharged. This is the fashion, in which the living truth of the gospel — has been woven into artificial expression by church dogmatists. ⫠ — The most valuable point of this doctrine of the atonement, is the view of divine justice which it presents, — and toward this most ... What is there in the nature of God or the nature of things — to make it necessary that divine ☒ forgiveness

of men, should wait, and depend upon, this ~~confine~~ —
~~Suppose~~ men had been justly doomed to everlasting
~~torment~~ — Might not God, if he had ~~chosen~~ chosen
have released them from ~~that doom~~ — just as well
before, as after Christ's work? — If a King, being
~~sued~~ sued for mercy by one ~~who~~ was under ~~sentence of~~
death, should consent that ~~the~~ the culprit might live in case
another should die for him, — ~~would that~~ be considered
a manifestation rather of justice or mercy? —
The doctrine of the atonement declares ~~proposes~~ that God
to be ~~true to himself~~ must ~~enforce~~ justice — But the
claims of justice are ~~satisfied~~, when the punishment
falls ~~broken then~~ upon the head of the guilty, — It is
divine mercy — not divine ~~justice which accepts~~ even that
sacrifice made by Christ — in place of man's endless

technical satisfaction of his claim. — "The quality of mercy is not strained." — A merciful God needs not to have the gift of eternal life wrung from him by the spectacle of guiltless misery. — In its endeavour to establish a compromise between divine justice and mercy, this doctrine contradicts both. — That is not justice which permits the guilty to escape in consideration of suffering voluntarily borne by the innocent, nor is it mercy, which only forgives sin when something like an equivalent for the whole penalty has been paid. — From this impeachment, a defender of the current doctrine can only take refuge in the assertion that God did all it was possible to do for man under the circumstances. — If we were dealing with some incidental fact or event this answer might suffice. But we are

make Him - like the old pagan Deities, subject to an overruling fate, -- So glaring are the inconsistencies of this doctrine - when the atonement of Christs death is represented as the necessary satisfaction of divine justice, - that the more liberal minds belonging to the old school of thought - have deserted that basis. They acknowledge that God might have been satisfied - and might have forgiven man's sin without Christs agony and death, - but hold that for the purpose of illustrating his justice - he chose that Jesus should suffer for all - as if God had feared that if he allowed ~~them~~ free - they would abuse his clemency. - They must be made to pay something - in order to convince them that the law still retained its terrors, -- So a magistrate who had sentenced an offender to receive a hundred lashes,

the clutches of the law. -- But here again the fatal objection is that the lash falls not upon the guilty but the guiltless. — Such an illustration of justice is either needless, or powerless. — ~~to~~ upon a mind so hardened as to need an exhibition of divine wrath, the spectacle of another suffering in his place would have no effect, — In order to inspire him with any terror of the law, the punishment must fall upon his own head, -- On the other hand, those souls which are sensitive and sympathetic enough, to be moved by the sight of another's anguish, — do not need that spectacle to put them in mind of the dreadful pain which follows guilt. — On this theory that Christ's death was designed to illustrate the terrors of divine justice, it is ~~on~~ sort of mockery, meaningless, and is then a ~~needless~~ exhibition of suffering. —

Now nothing is plainer than that the world is full of various suffering, — The innocent are

wrong doing — and in order to set others one ...
their sins — must take much sorrow for himself —
If the doctrine of the atonement were used simply
to symbolize or illustrate that fact — no one would find
fault with it — But We know that in an imperfect
state of being, the fortunes of good and bad are so
bound up together, that the good must often suffer for
no fault of their own — We reverence the great
hearted men and women — who for the sake of helping
their fellow creatures — cheerfully take upon themselves the
burdens borne by the sinful and unfortunate — We can
believe that God delights in this voluntary sacrifice of
self — and purposely leaves room for its exercise. But
it is an affront to the moral sense to declare that
justice demands — or is illustrated by vicarious
suffering — The cross is a symbol which God
may well unite with men to honor; since it
stands for the highest of which a human

Still it is undeniable that men have felt, there was some greater significance than this, to be attached to Christ's life and death, — They have seen in him not only an exhibition of the highest and most [heroic] virtue — but [...] the center of some almost [magical] or mystical influence — which put forth [...] at [...] in new attitudes [...] such toward the [...]. — Men's hearts are is often wiser than their heads, — [and] it is worth while to [...] [...] in this [...] of the atonement, — [...] is [...] root of [...] upon which the mind is instinctively laid to [grasp] — and which ought not to be confounded with the intellectual

There are two ways in which the old doctrine represents the influence of Christ as acting, — first. to satisfy God, and secondly to remove from man, his overwhelming load. — It is easy to show that Jesus could not have rendered to God that precise satisfaction — and or lifted from man that particular burden — which theologians have supposed that he gave and removed, — But it does not follow that mens feeling about the truth has gone astray — because their intellects have failed so sadly to provide for it satisfactory definitions, —

It has been the christian feeling, from the time of the disciples to the present day, that after Jesus had lived upon the earth — God regarded it with new interest and favor, — and not only is that feeling reasonable — but it must inevitably result from any high appreciation of the moral grandeur of Christs soul. — Suppose you had been for weeks and months — watching and caring for a window plant — which could not be

another, promising bud unfolding, only to disclose some fatal blight or defect – should you not after a time become discouraged? – and ____ at length one complete and beautiful flower did open in the sunlight – should you not feel a newly awakened interest in your plant, after it had shown what it was capable of producing? Why may we not suppose that the Creative mind had ____ ____ and waited for the appearance of the perfect human soul, – So hailed its appearance with joy – and so experienced a new ____ of love, for the race of men! – If in our ____ regard, humanity is exalted in the life of ____, – if it ____ ____ the possibilities of human ____ illustrated through him – add worth and

has grown discouraged waiting for Christs advent — nor could he have been relieved by Christs triumph over every form of evil, as if he had been uncertain of the issue, — But granting this, ~~must we suppose that~~ to the divine mind there is no ~~distinction between~~ the possible and the actual, ~~and that~~ he derives no pleasure from beholding ˄[in visible outward forms] what has hitherto existed only in his thought? ~~his own actual and visible body form?~~ Assuredly we may believe, that when ~~God saw for it first time~~ his full idea of man made flesh and blood, ~~He~~ felt a new joy in the work of his hands. — Is it now alone who is

seeking to mirror itself in created forms — take
pleasure in the birth of that ~~great human~~ soul
which is its ~~most~~ ripest creation and most
perfect symbol? — This then I take to be the root
of the Christian feeling — that the life of Christ — in
some way illumes ~~the attitude~~ of God toward man,
The notion ~~that~~ Jesus ~~paid off~~ God's claim against
humanity — and so appeased his wrath, is ~~only~~ a
very clumsy interpretation of this feeling, — a rude
~~guess~~ of the ~~half barbarous~~ mind — at the meaning
of intuitive perceptions much wiser than its own
understanding. — Jesus ~~did~~ we may believe — did
change the ~~divine~~ feeling — he won for all mankind
a larger measure of the divine love — ~~But~~ But he
did this simply by fulfilling the ~~divine purpose~~ as
man had never fulfilled it before. not by discharging
~~in the~~ his own person — the worlds whole debt of

have a longer right to live — than before they had known Christ? —
that in the sight of God they and all men had been made
more precious — by this great life that had spoken their
longings and borne their forms, — All that they said about
being bought by a price, and redeemed by his blood, means I
suppose that they felt God regarded them with new favor, for
Christ's sake, — How could they help feeling this? Jesus
had opened to them a new world of meaning in human
life — Under a poor light you may stand before the work
of some great master of painting and find it only a
flat mass of colors — But let in the sunlight upon it,
and this painted surface opens in a real perspective
through which the eye wanders in for distant mountains
and clouds — So under the light which Christ had
shed upon their experience — what had before been to his disciples a

suddenly acquired so much new worth in their own eyes
should seem to them of greater value in the sight of
God? and were they not right? If we conceive of
God as having any delight in the work of his hands—
must we not think that ~~the infinite mind thrilled~~
with a ~~new joy~~ because of the new perfection
which shone back from some ~~earth to heaven~~ the
mind of Christ? —

The other source of the ~~~~ astonishment
is the feeling that Jesus lifted from the souls of men
~~some burden~~. A burden of ~~~~ inherited guilt the
~~~~ ; but that again is only the
~~interpretation~~ put by theologians upon a feeling much
older than ~~themselves~~ or their theories. — Christ's
~~~~ was ~~~~ came to fulfill, not to
destroy, and Paul ~~taught~~ although it is often
exceedingly subtle and difficult to state, seems to
have been that Jesus ~~~~ men free from bondage
~~~~ the ~~~~ — It was the ~~~~ of ~~~~

to external power and authority - which seems removed -
for one thing,- and this he did not by completing any
bargain with the Almighty - but by awakening in
the souls of men new spiritual faculties which
rendered them independent of outward control. --

Whatever its explanation may be, the truth is
that men did "breathe with freer breath" - after Christ's
advent,- some weight had been taken from their
spirits. - The early christians think and act and
speak with a certain buoyancy and elasticity of
soul- very strongly marked in comparison with the
sombre and half despairing mood into which the
world of their day had for the most part fallen, --
and that has been to some extent a permanent
characteristic of Christian life, - one not to be
altogether explained I think - by the prevalent
Christian theories,- For though men believe that
the fall of Adam entailed upon the race a fe-

their sense of such danger and release - cannot be very lively - Even Paul's thought, though perfectly true, does not go quite far enough to explain why the Church since his day - should have kept its triumphant sense of new freedom through Christ, - For experience shows how soon men forget the tyranny from which they have escaped, and in how short a span of time this new liberty becomes old and stale, - Christians of to day ... the appreciation of what it meant to be in bondage to the Jewish Law, - and their lightness of heart cannot be well attributed to their grateful

But perhaps the word responsibility used in its popular sense comes as near the right word as any. — In one way the growth of the soul only serves to increase its sense of responsibility — by showing it how much depends upon its own action — and what far reaching results in its own and the future of other lives — it has power to control — But in another way spiritual progress tends to destroy this sense — by revealing to the soul the great organic whole (of which it forms a part,) and teaching it that instead of an isolated entity — dependent wholly upon its own resources — it is watched over — provided for — and controlled by a power infinitely wiser than itself, — ——————— Now we all know, do we not, that far more than any strain of work — it is the weight of anxious care — which breaks down the spirit — and wears out the life, — Of the various worldly employments which engage our attention, there are

those which put upon the individual the heaviest cares
and responsibilities. — A great many men, we say, break
down because they are overworked. — It would be far
more accurate [to say] victims of over-work — over-
worry. — The capacity of any healthy mind for work
is almost boundless, — In prosperous times — you shall
see men managing vast enterprises and interests —
[taxing] their working faculties continuously from
the [dawn till] — and doing this year after year
without injury of any kind, — But let these
stay men overcast with threats of disaster, — let it
become so difficult to conduct their ventures
to a successful issue — that the fear of ruin slams
them continually in the face — and you shall see that
[of this experience], count with their as years)
[works] — so swiftly will age and decay
creep upon them, — — So again think on people
of leisure — upon whom no demand for work
is made — who must yet bear a load of

any amount of labor, — and when people of active pursuits but with no special care, actually seem to grow young in the midst of their toil. these people — with nothing in particular to do, and a burden of real or fancied responsibilities to bear — will often speedily exhaust or imbalance their mental powers, — When the wheel is well balanced and nicely adjusted upon its bearings it makes little difference whether it revolves fifty or five hundred times per minute, — But — hang a heavy weight — upon one side of it, or around its bearings till they pinch, and even the strain of a very moderate motion will soon break the wheel —
centre

and uncertainty regarding Jehovah. — The Jew felt himself surrounded by a capricious will — which might seize upon his slightest failure to comply with the requirements of the law — and make it the pretext for sending upon him the worst calamities. — Then an certain seas in crossing which the mariner must be constantly upon his guard against sudden squalls, which with hardly a moment's warning fell upon him out of a cloudless sky, — He cannot set his sails as in other waters, with any assurance that the wind will hold in one quarter from now to hour but must be prepared to see them taken aback by an sudden and instant change, In such constant apprehension of what God might send to them, did the people of Christ's day live, and this it was that made for them a load of terrible responsibility. — What Paul meant by the bondage to law — was not merely the irksomeness of observing its manifold requirements, — It was rather the feeling of obligation which so tyrannized over

particular. ~~felt to be~~ thought himself in danger of the

the vast penalties with which almighty power would

visit him, — The disciples rejoiced in their liberty, —

not alone because of the trouble which it cost to observe the

law — but because ~~they had~~ escaped this galling sense of

responsibility to a capricious deity, —— It was this weight

which Jesus lifted, not only from the mind ~~of the Jew~~

but from the Christian consciousness ~~of all time~~, — The

Christian of to day is not obliged to go back 1000

years — to ~~find out~~ discover what that tyranny was, from which

Jesus released his immediate followers; — He finds it in

the world which he inhabits; he sees men so driven

and worried by their ignorance of the forces which

rule their destiny, He himself falls back ~~from time~~

to time into a mood of such timorous uncertainty that

he dreads as strongly as he hopes in what ~~scene~~ God

~~I shall receive~~ ~~the~~ ~~future~~, — Men to day, play

with circumstances as gamblers play with dice,

turn of <del>the</del> events, — <del>They</del> They live beneath a providence which may favor them, — or may at any moment smite him with a sudden tempest, —— Speculation is .. in the very air, and men speculate in religious and moral realities as <del>they speculate</del> in cotton or wheat, — They <del>think</del> they may sin to almost any extent and escape punishment, or <del>they may</del> for ^some very <del>slight offense</del> - call down upon <del>themselves</del> a <del>heavy judgment</del>, — They simply take <del>the</del> chances, and live as underneath a <del>providence of</del> power ^which has no <del>certain law of action</del> ——
<del>chance</del>, — It is this fact which explains why men grow <del>prematurely</del> old, and why every mad house is crowded <del>overflowing</del>; for the responsibilities thus put upon <del>the</del> mind are heavier than it can bear, — It is the weight, ^that is of all others <del>most oppressive</del>; this feeling of <del>the</del> ^soul which knows not God, that it is nothing but an adventurer in the world, with only chance and ^its own wits to depend upon, —— When <del>the</del> one is <del>in</del> ^it rides a sea - across which no steady tread ——

gales hold sway, one ~~feels~~ feels a responsibility, which not only demands unceasing watchfulness - but inspires a constant dread. — To us then - and to all generations - Jesus speaks as he did to his Jewish disciples, - bidding us know, that God forces more steadily and ceaselessly forward along the paths he has ordained. — — He tells us of a providence which is over us as a father's care, — of a God who shares with us life's responsibilities, — of a great stream - not ~~a~~ of fate, but of love — which if we will but trust ~~it~~ and work with its current bears our lines along to a fixed and certain destiny. He lifts the leaden pall from our spirits — by raising our eyes to that power enthroned in the heavens, which has made us what we are — and with which rests the burden of responsibility for the unknown future. Though the wind of the spirit blows when it listeth. and we cannot tell whence it comes or whither it goes. he makes us feel that

and that if we ~~seek~~ trim our sails to catch its
gentle influence - ~~it with~~ we may wake and sleep in
peace - ~~knowing~~ that we are being wafted to some
far away haven of rest, -

The heart of truth in the Christian doctrine
of an atonement - is that Christs ~~suffering~~ perfections
won from God a new regard for the humanity which
they ~~recalled~~ and adorned, ~~and~~ while his influence
over men removed from their spirits the weight
of ~~suffering~~ from which had bowed them prostrate
before the Deity, - That was the "satisfaction" he
rendered to God, - this the "Curse" ~~he~~ washed
out from ~~the~~ life by his blood, -- When
we reach this kernel of the doctrine, it explains
to us - as the doctrine in its popular form cannot -
why Christianity has poured into life nobility and
peace, - Indeed its dogma as it is commonly
~~preached~~ tends to degrade and belittle the soul, -

that we are — our hope of heaven hinges upon a commercial transaction in which we pay nothing and receive all the benefits?— But spite of this repulsive form, Christian feeling has always found in this doctrine — a deeper meaning than the intellect ~~has thus defined~~ It has ~~become~~ that in the sight of God every human life is made to share the life of Christ and through ~~trust~~ in him and all spiritual powers it has been led to lay down its burden of anxieties and responsibilities at the foot of God's throne, — And this explains too why the cross has become the great Christian symbol, and why so much power has been ascribed to ~~Christ~~ Christ's death ~~~~— It is no explanation of ~~of~~ the world's ~~of~~ estimate of the scene on calvary to say that the guilt of ages was atoned for by the anguish then suffered, The truth is that Christ's death was the seal of his life, — ~~&~~ All his greatness then comes into view, ~~and~~ All his career centers and culminates in his heroic death, — It was that which so stamped his image and his truth upon the hearts of men, — and then shone out in full glory, all ~~so then else~~ his wonderful peace and trust, —

influence has carried the human
confidence and [illegible] this d-
-with has thus brought [illegible] and
[illegible] a closer [illegible] it-
[illegible]. Surely this is a [illegible]
[illegible] of the adoration [illegible]
[illegible] has lavished upon it. -
[illegible] of the [illegible] theories - by [illegible]
it has tried to [illegible] spiritual

serious harm. If we laugh at these men themselves, the Christian consciousness has every age seen more than it could describe ... a deeper truth ... it could do,

It is for us — not to ridicule the past because of its intellectual weakness — interpret to this world — better how Church can make plain — the secret meanings of wonderful spiritual movement named ...

In so doing we shall do best to ... the full development of humanity's higher powers — and shall take the only way ... the power of ... can ... brother — as ... an idea of ... which ... formed doctrine only greatly represent ... positively permits. and they cannot ...

... is not a saviour in whom the world will
... ... , ... Christ who
... ... on ..., and makes
them feel that for his sake the Infinite Mercy
bows closer to their needs — this is the Christ
who has been ignorantly worshipped — and who
being declared to the world — shall yet stand as
the head of a Church — which more fully
appreciates his beauty and his strength. —